Wonders of Creation

Modern science in the Torah

Levi Tsehmeister · Nati Ben David · Avraham Nativ

Introduction

Since the beginning of childhood, curiosity derives us to learn and explore our surroundings.
We live in a fascinating world, where amazing things happen. From the wonders of the human body to the mysteries of the outer space.
Our children, and also adults, want to understand how the world works and how these amazing things around us are happening.
This curiosity is the foundation for humanity prosperity and development, and creating a better world with this knowledge.

The Torah-Bible is the foundation of the humanity morality and core values. The Torah-Bible Stories we read every week, are full of various topics from the world of science and nature, and directly connected to our everyday life, and deeds.

In this unique book, we will connect between the weekly Torah-Bible portions, to the most recent scientific knowledge. This bond will enable us to understand the Torah-Bible stories more deeply, perceive the meaning of our tradition and heritage relevance to our modern life.
In the book, we will explore the outer space to understand if Abraham would be able to count the stars as God asked him. We will go deep into the earth to understand how the stones got to the priest clothing's, and go into the yeast bacteria to know what the difference between Hametz (leaven) and Matzah is.
We will learn a variety of fields as medicine, technology, engineering, history, and more, all directly from the bible stories.

The book was written with the support of many scientists, doctors, etc. and bible teachers as well, to let the reader have the most precise knowledge and be loyal to the orthodox way of studying the bible. In every chapter, the Torah-Bible and science fertilization will derive an educational value to take to our everyday lives.

We would like to thank our supporters who made this book come true.
We wish you joyful reading, encouraging curiosity to explore the wonders of the Torah-Bible and the world we one.

In memory of
Zwi Zeev Ben Moshe Menachem OBM
Professor Harry Friedmann
To whom Torah and science were a guiding light

Contents

"Next time remove the hat before the X-ray"

The Special Mysterious Light

> **And G-d called the light Day and to the darkness he called Night.**

On the first day G-d created light. It came before the land, water, plants, and animals because these things need it to exist. Light is what gives life to the world. Can we imagine our world without light?

What exactly was the light that was created on the first day? After all, the sun, the moon, and the stars were all created on the third day and we know that our light comes from our sun. So where did the light of the first day come from?

Our Sages teach us that the light of the first day was a special light that G-d set aside for the future for the benefit of the pious. Let's try to have a better understanding of what light is and then perhaps we'll have a slightly better understanding of what this "special light" is.

Light allows us to be able to see things. The daylight that illuminates our sky in the daytime comes from the sun. Besides this light, we can also receive light from candles and table lamps. Wherever light shines we are able to view and distinguish a multitude of colors.

Do you think that it is possible that there exists light that we can neither see, nor sense? Is it possible that such a light exists?

Everyone has had the opportunity to take a picture with a camera. A standard camera draws in reflective light and projects it onto a screen. A different type of camera that is used in hospitals is called an X-ray machine. It is used to take pictures of the bones inside our bodies.

How is this possible? After all, we are not able to see our bones with our bare eyes? What type of mysterious light reflects off our bones into this type of camera?

Light is a wave of energy. Similar to the waves of the ocean, light comes in small and large waves, short and long waves. The light that we are able to see is only a very tiny portion of the vast array of waves that exist in nature and in fact there are light waves that we can not distinguish at all. Radio waves and telephone waves, for example, are waves that constantly surround us and yet we can not see them. All of these waves are similar and just differ in wave length.

The sun projects light waves and heat waves

Our eyes are only able to detect light waves of very specific wave lengths. Each one of those wave lengths creates a specific recognizable color. They range from purple to red. Wave lengths that are either longer or shorter than this range are not visible to our eyes.

Animals have the capacity to see beyond the capabilities of man. Snakes, for instances, can see heat waves that humans are incapable of seeing. The types of light that we can not see have many usages. X-ray machines, for example, project "X" light waves that have very short wave lengths that can pass through our bodies, but not through our bones. Thus, this type of external camera can penetrate through our skin and flesh and take a picture of just our bones. This is how we are able to determine if a bone is broken.

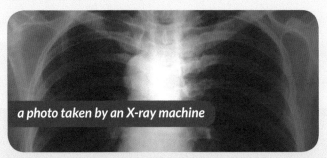

a photo taken by an X-ray machine

We all heat up food now-a-days using a microwave. What do you think causes the food to warm up? It's not the light bulb that's inside the microwave.

Inside the microwave there are invisible light waves that heat up the liquid within the food as it is passing through. That is how the meal is cooked.

Radio waves and telephone waves are very long waves and through them we are able to send messages and broadcasts very long distances. These waves have the ability to penetrate through houses and other obstacles and thus they are perfect for transferring communications very far distances very quickly. Literally at the speed of light.

Our sun as well radiates both visible and invisible light. The invisible light can damage our skin and therefore we place on sunscreen to protect us against it.

The different types of light wave that exist were discovered in the last 200 years through the efforts of several different scientists. For example, Wilhelm Conrad Röntgen who invented the X-ray machine and Heinrich Hertz who discovered the microwaves that heat things.

In recent years space researchers have discovered that besides the twinkling of the stars that our visible to our eyes, there are also many other invisible waves that reach us from space such as Gamma and Micro waves. By studying these waves we are able to determine an abundant of new facts pertaining to distant stars and what they are made of.

Israeli radars that detect radio waves from satellites

We see that G-d created light waves of various types that help us in many ways and forms. Imagine if our eyes could see all these waves. We'd be able to see how telephone conversation arrive. We'd also be able to see the waves that broadcasts our internet and the heat that comes out of the oven. That would be a very special gift that is better kept for unique individuals. Perhaps this is the "special light" that was created on the first day of creation!

For us, it's enough that we are able to see normal light and colors and when the sun sets we give our eyes rest and sink into a deep sleep.

Interesting facts

There are special night vision goggles that allow us to see objects at night by viewing the heat waves that emanate off of them in the same manner that snake are able to see. These goggles are used by the military to expose enemy vehicles and personnel by viewing the heat that they radiate.

Sun rays move at extremely fast speed. 300,000 kilometers per second! None-the-less, it take a full 8 minutes for sun rays to reach Earth because the sun is very far away from us.

Telephone communication between the space shuttle and Earth can take many hours. Imagine how an astronaut tries to communicate with his family.

The Race to the Sky

The babylonians wanted to build a tower who's apex would reach the heavens

G-d was not happy with the Babylonians and therefore confused their language. At that point the people couldn't understand each other and therefore couldn't proceed in building the tower.

Our sages from the time of the Talmud visited the ruins of Babylon and related over what they saw. The ruins that still remained from the tower was so high that whoever stood at the top of it and looked down viewed humans as if they were ants!

Can you imaging how high the tower could have been!

How can a tower be build so high?

Even after the tower of Babylon people continue to build very tall building and skyscrapers. Around 4,000 years ago the Egyptians built huge pyramids that were considered the tallest constructions for thousands of years. Their height was 140 meters (the height of a 40 story building) and they are still standing until today.

In the last couple of hundreds of years they have successfully build skyscrapers that have towered well beyond the height of the pyramids and there is a constant race to built the tallest skyscrapers in the world.

About a hundred years ago they began to build many large towers that exceeded well beyond what was previously achieved. Every couple of years towers are built that break the previous world record. The Eiffel Tower in France, skyscrapers in New York, and the Taipei 101 in Taiwan. In 2010 construction of the Burj Khalifa in Dubai was completed. It's heights rises to an astonishing 828 meters (163 stories high)! As of today it remains the tallest building in the world. Has this ended the competition? Definitely not!

In the city of Jeddah, Saudi Arabia, a taller skyscraper is being built that is expected to be completed in 2018 and is supposed to reach a height of 1000 meters. It's interesting to note who's already trying to surpass it. It sounds easy, no? All in all, all you need is a few more bricks, building material, and some taller cranes. In truth, it's not so simple. For the construction engineers who design such humongous edifices there is a lot of challenges and problems to overcome.

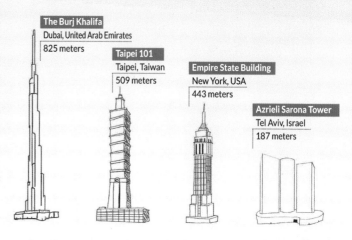

The Burj Khalifa
Dubai, United Arab Emirates
825 meters

Taipei 101
Taipei, Taiwan
509 meters

Empire State Building
New York, USA
443 meters

Azrieli Sarona Tower
Tel Aviv, Israel
187 meters

The First Challenge: Wind

At ground level wind is not very strong. However, the higher you climb the stronger the wind force gets. At an altitude of several hundred meters the wind force is extremely strong. Therefore, skyscrapers need to be built out of very strong material in order to withstand the extreme wind force (also referred to as wind load) existing at such heights. In Taiwan, for example, there are occasionally strong tornadoes, which were a cause for concern for the designers of Tower 101 in Taipei, the capital city. In order to overcome this problem they installed huge weights that can move from side to side in order to balance the building in stormy weather.

The Second Challenge: Stability

Anyone who has ever built a tower from blocks knows that the wider and more solid the foundation is the higher and or stable the tower can be built.

The base of a skyscraper need to be wide and large and the foundations need to be solid and dug very deep within the ground.

The Third and Most Amazing Challenge: The Elevator

In order to implement an elevator system so high up it's necessary to have very thick cables that are extremely long and can reach all the way to the top. Installation of such an elevator adds a lot of complexity to such a high tower. For instance, it would be very unpleasant to reach an office on the 114th floor and find out that the elevator is stuck.

Already many years ago engineers were contemplating how to build a tower that will reach into space. This tower is also called a "space elevator". Through the means of this tower it will be possible to reach space without needing a rocket ship. This tower will need to be made out of a very strong material in order to withstand the stress and forces that will be applied upon the space elevator.

Tower 101 in Taipei

Mankind still hasn't successfully found material that strong. However, scientists speculate that in the future it will be possible to go up in such elevators far out into outer space.

We all want to grow and reach as high as possible and from the towers we can learn a few lessons:

Above all, one's foundations must be strong. Our sages teach us that before all else one must act with proper conduct and have good character traits. These are the foundations necessary. When the foundations are strong it is much easier to proceed in all other aspects of Judasim.

In order to attain great heights one must know how to stand strong against the "winds" and difficulties. However, at times it's important to be bending, yielding and flexible (literally like the apex of a tower). Otherwise, one may come to break. This is liken to what our sages say, "a person should always be soft as a reed and not hard as a cedar tree".

In conclusion, there is no boundaries to what we can accomplish. In every aspect of the world there is always what to learn and apply.

Interesting facts

💡 A stone thrown from a very high tower or plane will increase velocity as it falls. However, once it reaches 200 km per hour it will remain at that speed since air resistance prevents it from falling faster.

💡 Robert Alan Eustace, a senior executive at Google, set the record for highest free fall. He jumped from a gas balloon from a height of 42 kilometers high reaching the edge of the stratosphere. At such height one needs a space suit and oxygen tanks. One also obviously needs a parachute as well.

💡 When we stand here on the ground the Earth appears to be flat. However, if we observe from the top of the highest skyscraper we can distinguish the roundness of the Earth's globe.

Parshat Noach

The Stars and Granules of Sand

G-d blessed Avraham with a very special blessing.

Avraham was already an old man, 99 years of age, and still remained childless. He was already assuming that he was not going to have any children. Therefore, Hashem reassured him by blessing him that he would have many offspring, as plentiful as the granules of sand in the world. Afterwards, Hashem took him outside his tent in order to have him look up at the heavens and Hashem told him, "Just like it's impossible to count the stars because there are so many, so too your children and descendants will be too numerous to count."

In your opinion, why did Hashem bless Avraham that his children will be abundant like the sand and the stars? Which blessing is the more important and more significant one, to be as abundant as the stars or the granules of sand? What do you think?

In order to answers these question we first have to answer another question?

What are there more of in the world, stars in the heavens or grains of sand along the beaches?

This is a very strange question indeed and perhaps impossible to solve. After all, is it possible to count all the grains of sand in the ocean? Can one enumerate the stars in the heavens? Although it will be very difficult to give an exact answer, none-the-less we will attempt to give answer based on a rough estimation.

Let's first start with the start in sky.

If we stare up into the sky at night we can count how many stars there are. However, if we leave the city and go to a place that is very secluded we will be able to see many more stars that we couldn't see before. Now, if we look up at the sky using a telescope we will see a vast array of stars the are not visible to the naked eye.

Not so long ago, in the year 1990, America set into orbit a unique telescope satellite that they named

"Hubble" that is able to see extremely far into space. With the aid of this telescope scientists are able to scan every part of outer space and take pictures of it. They then examine these pictures very carefully. Every speck of light in a picture can be a lone star or a cluster of stars that are very close to one another. They can even be a vast constellation of stars which due to the great distance from us appear as a single spot of light.

A picture taken from the Hubble telescope)

Hubble telescope in space

In this manner, scientists are able to estimate how many stars exist in the universe that are within our present capabilities to see. According to scientific estimations the number of stars is astronomical and is difficult to calculate or even to comprehend. However, with the aid of sophisticated computers it's possible to calculate the number of stars to be at least a trillion trillions. That being a 1 followed by 24 zeros!

1,000,000,000,000,000,000,000,000

There is no question that number is astronomical!

So now, what about the grains of sand? On the beaches alone lie a tremendous amount sand! Could it be that on the beaches lie more grains of sand than the amount of stars that exist in the heavens above?

It is possible to estimate how much sand is on an average strip of beach that extends for a kilometer (approx. 0.621 mile) and has a width of 35 meters (approx. 114.8 feet) and a depth of 10 meters (approx. 32.8 feet). If we estimate a granule of sand to be about a fifth of a millimeter (approx. 0.02 inch) then such a coastline with consist of 125 billion grains of sand. This is a huge number for sure!

We will multiply this number by the number of beaches worldwide (which can easily be seen on a map of the world). Of course, not all beaches are filled with sand. However, like we've stated prior, it is not so important to have an exact figure. We are just looking for a rough estimate.

Such calculation will come out to be a huge number of granules of sand; One million trillion grains of sand! That's a 1 followed by 18 zeros:

1,000,000,000,000,000,000

Although this may be a very large number, none-the-less it's tiny in comparison to the amount of stars visible in photographs taken from space.

That means to say that our estimation of the amount of stars in the heavens is greater than the amount of grains of sand on all the coastal lines on Earth. Amazing, isn't it? The sand seems to be so abundant and yet there are actually more stars!

At this point we can now understand why Hashem blessed Avraham that his descendants would be as numerous as the granules of sand whose abundance is easily noticeable.

However, the more important and significant blessing is the blessing to be as numerous as the stars. At first glance, it does not appear that there are so many stars. However, upon a deeper examination it is clear that there are a tremendous amount beyond compare. Besides this, their power and intensity that is hidden within them is very great.

There is a profound message that we can take from the sand and the stars.

Granules of sand are very tiny. However, when placed together they form vast stretches of grandiose beaches. Also, when we look up to the heavens the view of all the stars together give a sense of it's awesomeness.

So too by us, each and everyone of us has tremendous value. However, our essence is truly revealed when we are united as one!

Interesting facts

💡 Have you ever considered how many water particles, called atoms, are in just two drops of water? The answer is an incredibly large number: 1 with 20 zeros after it. That means to say that it is nearly as many as the stars in the heavens! We don't think about that when we are drinking a cup of water, do we?

💡 The stars that we see in the sky are stars that shine bright just like our sun. In fact, many of them are actually clusters of thousands of stars that just seem to us as one bright spot.

💡 Our Earth is not a shiny star, but rather a planet that does not shine. Even with telescopes it is difficult to distinguish planets that are not luminous. Thus, it is no easy task to find in space planets liken to our Earth.

Dead Sea Salt

The people of Sodom and Gomorrah established laws that forbade providing help and assistance to one another and whoever dares to give food to a guest would be punished immediately.

The people of Sodom and Gomorrah did not like outsiders coming and asking for food and a place to sleep. You wouldn't want to live in a place like this, right?

Lot, Avraham Avinu's nephew, lived with his wife in Sodom. He would always invite guests just like he learned from Avraham even though no one else in Sodom practice this way. However, his wife acted in accordance to the laws of Sodom and was not willing to give the guests anything, even salt! Hashem saw how bad the people of Sodom were and therefore he sent angels to destroy the city. Moments before the destruction, the angels evacuated Lot's family from the city. However, during their escape Lot's wife looked back and turned into a pillar of salt. Yes, this really happened!

How come Lot's wife became a pillar of salt?

Our sages explain that Lot's wife was punished because she did not want to invite guests and even a pinch of salt she did not want to give.

However, we still need to understand why she became a pillar of salt and not a pillar of bread or milk? After all, Lot's wife wasn't willing to honor her guests even with bread or milk.

What do you think? In order to answer this question let's learn about salt.

What is salt?

Our world is composed of many different materials: Water, earth, rocks, gases, metals, etc. If we explore what each material is composed of we will discover that all materials in our world are compounds composing of a mixture from 118 substances referred to as Elements.

Since the creation of the world, various processes have taken place in nature such as rainfall, snowfall, volcanic eruptions, drying up of lakes and streams, etc.

These processes form compounds called Minerals. Minerals are nature's treasures that are located in different locations: In the ocean, on the mountains, and deep within the ground. Minerals are of extreme importance in our lives. Diamonds, for example, are one of the most well known minerals. Another mineral that is found in every house is salt, which is a compound of two elements: Sodium and Chlorine.

How come salt is such a necessity for us? Can we go without it?

The human body requires the element Sodium (one of the ingredients of salt). Sodium participates in the process of transporting substances into the cells of the body and removing them. Likewise, it's responsible for the proper functioning of the muscles and nerves. Even though salt (Sodium) is vital for proper bodily function, none-the-less, too much salt can be harmful to the body. How much salt must one consume?

For kids up to nine years of age it is recommended to consume up to 1.2 grams of sodium per day, which is less than three fourths a tablespoon a day. Frozen foods (such as bourekas and malawach) as well as processed foods (such as hot dogs and pastrami) have high quantities of salt. Did you know that salty snacks (bamba, bissli, potato chips, etc.) contain massive quantities of sodium? Even sweat snacks (cereal, cookies, and ketchup) contain large amounts of sodium. It's possible to know how much sodium is in every product by looking at the product label under "Nutrition Facts" for Sodium and see how much it contains. In order to minimize salt intake and to eat healthier it's preferable to eat home made food rather than to buy take out or processed foods. So too, it is better to eat less snacks which contains a lot of salt and replace them with fresh fruit. It's much healthier and better tasting.

How does salt come to our salt shakers? Where is it manufactured? Salt is produced in three ways:

The first method: Drying sea water. Anyone who's been at sea knows that it is very salty. How does the salt reach the sea? All streams and rivers flow into the sea. On the way they bring with them salt that is found on mountainous rocks. Some of the sea water evaporates into clouds and the salt remain behind in the sea; thus causing the sea to become salty. In order to extract the salt, the sea water gets drawn into shallow pools. Then the sun dries up the water and only the salt remains in these pools. Afterwards, the salt is collected and packaged for sale.

A salt wall at Mount Sodom

The second method: Mining underground for salt. This is practiced in many states in America and provinces in Canada where salt is found deep down in the ground.

The third method: Mountain quarrying. The are a few places in the world where there are salt mountains. These mountains are made of salt and in order to extract the salt these mountains must be quarried. Mount Sodom, which is near the Dead Sea, is the largest stockpile of salt in the world.

If so, which do you think is the easiest way to extract salt?

The obvious answer: Mountain quarrying! You don't need to search for the salt. All you need to do is come to the mountain with a shovel and start shoveling as much as you want.

Remember what we asked at first: Why did Lot's wife become a pillar of salt and not for example a pillar of bread?

Lot and his wife lived in Sodom. There, as mentioned, is Mount Sodom which is made up of a tremendous amount of salt. All that Lot's wife had to do is to take a little bit of salt that was waiting for her on the mountain and give it to her guests. As we saw earlier, the easiest way to obtain salt is from salt mountains. Almost no effort is required.

Now it is clearer why she received this specific punishment, isn't it? As a result of Lot's wife's stinginess and meanness, Hashem turned her into a pillar of salt, specifically salt!

Lot and his wife were blessed with an abundance of salt. Even though Lot's wife had a wealth of salt, none-the-less, she was not willing to give any of it away to their guests.

Each and every one of us is gifted with special talents: One of us may have spectacular artistic abilities, another may have a clear singing voice, and a third person excels in his studies or at playing ball. We have to contemplate on how we can use our unique abilities for the benefit of others and not to just keep them to ourselves. If we will seek to help one another our world will definitely become a much better place.

Interesting facts

💡 All the sacrifices in the holy temple required salt added to them. Our sages established that we use Dead Sea Salt specifically being that it is considered pure and of high grade. For this purpose there was a special chamber established in the holy temple to house the salt called the Lishkat HaMelach (the Salt Chamber).

💡 The Dea Sea is ten times saltier than the Mediterranean Sea. The reason for this is because the Dea Sea water remains idle and does not flow.

💡 The Dea Sea, which is near where Sodom was located, is the lowest place on Earth. It stands at approximately 400 meters below sea level.

400 Ancient Shekels

After Sarah's death, Avraham invested time and effort in order to attain a burial place for her.

He turns to Efron the Chiti who offers him his field for free. However, Avraham refused and insisted on paying. In the end of their verbal exchange, Avraham agrees to pay 400 shekalim for ownership of the Me'arat Hamachpela and it's surroundings in Hevron.

How much was that 400 shekalim really worth? Is the amount that Avraham paid equivalent to today's 400 Shekels? Today, with that amount, we can only buy a pair of shoes, a shirt, and a pair of pants. Does the value of coins change over time?

The history of trading

In order to understand the process, let's go back in time to find out how people have been involved in commerce from ancient times until today.

At first, it was accepted to use the method of "trade exchange". That means to say that people exchanged merchandise between themselves. For example, let's imagine one person was a shepherd and another was a farmer (Do you remember Kain and Hevel?). When the shepherd was in need of fruits, vegetables, flour or the like, he would acquire some from his friend, the farmer. In exchange, the shepherd would give the farmer from his animals (meat, wool, etc.) according to the farmer's needs. Everything according to what one took and what he had to offer in exchange.

Over time, people began to notice that it was becoming more and more difficult to evaluate between different goods. After all, one sheep could be worth a year's supply of cucumbers, which is not easy to transfer from one location to the next.

What is your opinion? Would you want to drag your cow all the way to another location in order to exchange it for a ton of apples?

In order to make commerce easier, it was decided to purchase goods using precious metals whose value would be determined by their weight; an ounce of gold, an ounce of copper, etc.

These nuggets of precious metals were called "bullion". Thus, payment for products were purchased with bullion. For example, a pound of flour might have been purchased with an ounce of copper.

The Introduction of Coins

Over time, bullion were replaced by coins. The coins were made from the same materials as the bullion. However, they were molded into various, more comfortable shapes.

Every region and empire had its own coins. How much do you think each coin was worth? Their value was based on their weight!

A gold coin that weighed 100 grams was worth 100 grams of gold. A silver coin that weighed 80 gram was worth 80 grams of silver.

Picture of old coins from the time of Julius Caesar and the revolt of Bar Kochva. Photo by: CNG COINS

Each country created its own currency with it own unique inscription and usually included images and designs distinctive to their region, such as the face of their king and the like. In wealthier countries, the coins were more valuable, because they were made from more expensive materials.

In the Torah, the shekel is mentioned very often. For example: In our parashah, it is mentioned in the story of Avraham and Efron. Elsewhere, it mentions the machatzit hashekel, which was donated to the temple. Many more examples can be cited as well. The shekel was an ancient weight, and the coin uniquely based on that weight was called a "shekel". In other words, the shekel is the name of the weight of the coin and it is also the name of the coin itself.

Returning to our original question: Is today shekel similar to the shekel of the bible?

Not at all! Over time, coins have changed completely. Nowadays, instead of using expensive materials, we have begun to use very cheap metals. If so, in your opinion, how do you think they determine the value of each coin?

In truth, there is no definitive answer.

Today, the value of the coin is not determined based on the material used, nor is it based on its shape. The decisive factor is much simpler:

A coin that is designed to represent a certain value is valued at that sum and a coin that is designed for a different value is valued at that sum. There are no basis to their value. Bank notes, as well, are printed representing different values with no relationship to the cost of the paper used. For example, how much does the paper of a two hundred shekels bill costs? Just a few Agorot. Thirty years after the state was establish it was decided to make the official Israeli currency the "Shekel". After time, they changed the currency to the "New Shekel" and that is the currency that is used until today.

The new shekel

When Avraham bought the Maarat Hamachpela in Hevron he invested a lot of money; 400 silver Shekels. It was worth a lot more than 400 shekels of today. Every shekel coin of that time, today would amount to a lot of money! It's value would be roughly 25,000 "New Shekels" per coin! Furthermore, those ancient shekels were made out of a unique gold and were excepted as currency in every country in the world. Avraham understood that in the future nations would come and claim that the caves of Machpelah do not belong to the Jewish people. He, therefore, purchased the site in front of a whole crowd at an unforgettable price in order that no one in the world would be able to question who acquired it and at what price. Avraham also knew that paying in cash would have a greater impact than any other means of transaction.

Avraham Avinu taught us that if we discover something of great importants, we should invest in it, even if it requires investing great effort, strength, time and/or money. Avraham concerned himself to find a respectful burial place for his wife Sara and he was also concerned for us, his children.

Interesting facts

💡 After the destruction of the Second Temple, Bar Kochva led a revolt against the Romans and tried to establish our own independent state. He wasn't successful in the end. However, he met enough success that he began minting coins to be used and called them the "Israeli Shekel".

💡 The shape of coins is usually round. However, there are coins that are oval in shape! These coins are elongated and used in various countries throughout the world.

💡 How many ribs does a five shekel coin have? Twelve ribs! Check it out for yourselves. This coin is the heaviest of all the coins in our wallets.

Parashat Toldot

Race for Water

Yitzhak, our forefather, lived in the dessert of Israel in an area where it rarely rained and where there were no nearby streams.

In order to obtain water, Yitzhak and his servants dug wells very deep in to the ground until they reached underground water. In contrast to the Philistines' failed attempts, whom were not able to find even a drop of water, Yitzhak was successful in finding water from wells time after time. The Philistines were jealous of him and drove him out of their land. In the end, however, the Philistines begged Yitzhak to return.

In our times, this story seems very strange to us being that nowadays it is very easy to obtain water. All we need to do is turn the handle of the faucet and water comes out. It wasn't always that easy, however.

How did they obtain water in the olden days?

During the times of the Torah and the Mishna, as well as from the middle ages until just a few decades ago, a lot of effort was needed in order to obtain even a few liters of water. It was easiest to live near a well or a river and draw water from it each time needed and bring it home. Laundering and bathing, were usually done in the river itself, so as not to have to carry water to another place. It seems simple, right? It turns out it was not so simple.

Sometimes there were no easy access to the water sources and sometimes the nearby river had dried up. Also, what did they do at night when people are afraid to go out in the dark? Furthermore, what did people

A well in the middle of the desert

do during very cold seasons? At times, they simply forewent the use of water unless it was an absolute necessity.

That's how life was like near natural sources of water. What did they do in places that were not close to the water sources? How did they obtain water?

The other populated areas can be divided into places where it rained frequently and places where rain was scarce. In both of these areas, it was necessary to exert more effort to attain water. In areas where it did not rain frequently they would use groundwater for drinking. This water laid below the surface of the ground and in order to reach it they would have to dig deep into the ground and hope they would hit water. In order to raise water from the well, they used a bucket and rope. This method of drawing water required great strength and skill. Would you go all the way out to a well just to fill a glass of water? Of course not! When they drew water they made sure to draw up enough water for drinking, cooking and even...

for bathing. (Yes, at that time showers were not yet invented).

In places where there was abundant rainfall, they dug deep pits and rain water would flow through various water ducts that led to the pits. The pits were plastered with lime, which is used as a sealing agent that prevents water from eroding the earthen walls of the pit.

In biblical times, canals also brought water from lakes, rivers, and other bodies of water directly to the cities. Thus, they needed to find water sources that existed at high altitudes since the nature of water is to flow from a higher place to lower place. If the down flow of water was not steep enough it would not reach the city. Therefore, during the excavations, one had to find the most convenient and quickest routes. At times, they even needed to tunnel through the mountains in order to insure constant flow of water. Does it sound complicated? Yes, it is really was!

Is there no other solution to transfer water from place to place? Also, when did they finally start using pipes?

The first ones to discover this method were the Romans who used pipes to transfer water to the multitude of bathhouses that were established throughout their empire. Throughout the ages this method was improved. However, the Romans were the ones who invented it.

With the establishment of the State of Israel, Mekorot, Israel's National Water Company, began planning on how to supply water to the entire country. Specifically, they were concerned with how to supply water to the southern half of Israel where there is hardly any water; for example the city of Beersheba. (Yes, that's the location where Isaac dug his wells). After a couple of years, they completed one of the largest projects in the history of the State: The National Water Carrier. With the assistance of very large pipes that are connected to the Kinneret, they were able to transfer water to almost every part of the country. From them, other pipes branch out carrying water to each building until it reaches the water faucet in your home.

The National Water Carrier, photographer: Iaam

Every drop of water counts.
There are places in the world that are not lacking water at all. The water flows there in abundance. However, Israel is located in an area where there are not too many sources of water available. Thank G-d, the world has evolved and today it is much easier to stream water. In addition, we have managed to preserve agriculture in the country and there are many parks and greenery that need a lot of water. Even so, we are limited to the amount of water that can be drawn. Therefore, it is vital to conserve as much water as possible. Bottom line, we must remember and not forget that the "keys" to rain are in G-d's hands.

Interesting facts

💡 The oldest and most famous water canal in Israel is called the Shiloah Tunnel (called Siloam Tunnel in English). King Hezekiah used it to transfer water from the Gihon Spring to Jerusalem within the walls of the old city about 3,000 years ago.

💡 What is there more of in the world, water or dry land? It may not look like it, but the majority of the Earth is covered with water; almost twice as much water than land. Look at a globe and check it out for yourself.

💡 Not only is the taste of water in every country different, but even the taste of their other drinks. This is because every country uses their own water in preparation for their drinks.

The Secret Defense Code

After twenty years of hard labor in Lavan's house, Yaakov wanted to start a new life with Rachel, Leah, and their children.

Yaakov requests from Lavan his salary for his hard work done throughout the years. Lavan agrees to pay Yaakov, especially after hearing Yaakov's suggestion. Yaakov suggests that he be paid in the form of receiving lambs the flock of sheep and Yaakov will separate his sheep from Lavan's. The sheep that have colored spots or brown spots will remain by Lavan and Yaakov will receive all the white sheep. Later, all the colored or brown spotted sheep and goats that will be born to Yaakov's flocks will belong to Yaakov, while those born white will go to Lavan. Lavan is enthusiastic and immediately agrees with the deal because he is sure that he will profit from the deal.

Why does Lavan think this way? How was Yaakov successful in profiting from all the flock?

The answer to the question is very simple. Lavan thought that if the colored and brown flock were not owned by Yaakov, there is no chance for his white flock to give birth to colored or brown ones. Usually, the children look similar to their parents. In addition, the white sheep that are owned by Yaakov will give birth to white lambs and Yaakov will need to give them over to Lavan, the father of Rachel and Leah.

If that is the case, what secret did Yaakov know that Lavan was not aware of? It appears that Yaakov knew of the genetic code.

In order to understand what the genetic code is, we need to travel deep inside our bodies to the smallest particles in it.

The human body and other living beings are combined of many tiny cells. Each group of cells form an organ in our bodies. For example, skin cells form skin and brain cells form... the brain. Within each cell there is a nucleus which contains within it a tiny coil called DNA. DNA is composed of a chain of different matter called genes and they determine our properties. That is, what will be the color of our hair, what color of eyes we will have. If we are going to be tall or short or fast or slow, or wide or narrow.

The National Water Carrier, photographer: laam

You have probably noticed that a definite feature that our parents have is very likely to pass to our children too. Tall parents will have a tall child and the color of the eyes will resemble the color of his parents eyes. Sometimes two parents with brown eyes will have a child with blues..how could that be?

Hereditary and body traits

about 150 years ago Scientists discovered the hereditary laws of how trait pass from parents to their children.It was discovered that we have two types of genes one asleep and one awake.A controlling gene determined how the organ in our body will look dormant and does not determine how the organ will look in our body.how he hides in our body.when the genes pass to the offspring the dormant gene may become the duodenum. The model of a man with brown eyes may have a dorman garden of blue eyes. so sometimes we see blue eyes parents sleeping.and suddenly the child woke up more than that if we look at the extended family,other children with blue eyes werebiten because this feature was raised with the family.

Now we will return to Jacob genetic genes

Like humans,sheeps and goats also have genes that determine the color of their fur.The aramaic son thought that if the sheep were white,Jacob would have nothing to gain.But Jacob understood the genetic herds and knew that the colors and points were also found,in the heavy white lions.They are simply dormant so their offspring can certainly have points and colors.and even more likely because the color scheme has a higher chance of being the dominant gene.

This is the reason that Jacob davened to hashem and request that it transform dormant attribute of points and colors into dominant features.In this way he could make a profit from Laban by giving him the news of his work.

Sometimes we think that we are certain that we should be one way or another and that our future will be written in advance.

However like the genetic coding, we alos have dormant forces that we do not know about. These forces can suddenly burst and suprise everyone. and we will never forget the unique gift we received that we have to turn to gd and ask him to guide us and suceed in our path just as Jacob prayed and received from heaven.

Interesting facts

💡 Twin children have the same genes.thats why one is similar to the second one. s their behaviour also the same? The new investigation shows that twins that were divided and didn't grow up in the same place they behaved similary and their areas of interested is similar. Some claim that a special gene was found amongst priests that passes between the patriarch of the family.

💡 Thus a simple examination of drops of blood or saliva from the mouth will enable us to find the connection between all the priest in the jewish people until the first priest Aharon hakohen.

💡 Even though the Jews are common throughout the world for long years of exile and the genetic baggage from the rest is due to the strict observance of the Jewish marriage.

I received a message

Old New Message

Yaakov our forefather is under a lot of tension.

This is the very first time that Yaakov is going to meet Eisav for the very first time since he ran away from him. Yaakov is interested to send his brother a message about peace and presents, how does presents reach his brother. If it had happened nowadays then Yaakov needed to call or send a message before the meeting.

In early days Yaakov decides to send angels as messengers and they will discover the real reason behind.

Why does Yaakov want to send messengers? Is there a real reason behind?

From then and nowadays people try to find ways to send each other messages because they leave far distances.

What would you do if you really need to ask for help?

Many people thought about lighting a bonfire. Many stories tell us about people that light a bonfire when they were strangled in a deserted island. This is in fact a favorite to attract attention. In the Past, fires have had other roles, such as the sanctification of the new month.

What does lighting fire have to do with sending messages and publicizing the new month?

Nowadays, each person has a calendar in their house and with its help they know when each holiday starts. In the past, when the temple existed, the Jewish court decided each month when rosh chodesh applies, and according to that they knew to celebrate the holidays. After sanctifying the new month, the jews of Israel and Babylonia had to be informed of the beginning of a new month in order for all the jews to celebrate the holidays at the same date. How was the new month publicized? After all Babylonia is 1000 kilometer away from Israel.

In order to pass the message, fires were made on top of the mountains, the distant jews who saw the fire also burned a bonfire on top of the mountain, thus, the announcement of the sanctification of the new month moved quickly from mountain to mountain until it reached the jews of the far Babylon.

In the past, amongst American Indians, lighting bonfires was a way of a communication between different tribes. They will light a bonfire and create clouds of smoke according to a code they all new. For example three successful clouds of smoke were sign of danger or call for help. Even today sailors and fly attendance always have a distillation or a smoke candle so they can call for help and mark where they are. Another way to deliver messages was through homing pigeons witch was used until not long ago.

Every settlement had a pigeon's blossom, the person who is in charge to send homing pigeons to neighbor countries. Before the state was established, that is to say in the time of the palmach and the idf there were unions of pigeons. The pigeons were like soldiers who specialized in transmitting messages between the army units with pigeons.

How come they used pigeons instead of any different type of bird?

Sending pigeons and not a different bird came from the pigeon nature to return to the loft they came from. Surprisingly, they remember the exact way from the bird house. For example in order to send a message from Tel Aviv to Jerusalem needed to take a pigeon with an attached massage to her leg and send it. After all she would end up on her way to Jerusalem.

In ancient times messengers were the most common way of transmitting messages. And an emissary in whom it was possible to relay, had to make an effort to carry out his mission effectively. And if the messages were secret, he kept her and did not transfer her another way. However, the transmission of a message with one messenger has a disadvantage. A single messenger might lose his way or his life and the message will not reach its destination.

Therefore, kings in the past were sending some messengers to pass one important message. Nowadays we receive messages throughout our phones radio and internet.

However, some of the message sending principals remain the same. The internet for example, is based on many computers that are connected and communicate with one another. Therefore the message that were sent throughout email always passing through a few computers, as in the days of the past sent several messengers to deliver one message. Meaning that the message would reach its destination even if the computer failed to transmit it.

Bonfires on the hills

In ancient times, when the king sent an emissary to notify the enemy, there was a risk that the enemy would capture the messenger and will not let him to return to his country.

When they sent a messenger to someone whom they don't get along with, they actually they put trust in him. That's how Yaakov treated Eisav. Yaakov respected Eisav and send messengers and expected the messengers to return safely. Perhaps, it was the expression of trust that made Eisav soften, and he returned the messengers

safely and gave up the war.

We also sometimes fight with friends. It happens when a friend doesn't treat us properly and we are angry with him and we want to punish our friend, but if we acostume to treat our friend with respect and derech erets, the friend would relies that he has been wrong. At the end he will regret his actions and there will be peace between us.

Interesting facts

💡 On the times of the Mishnah when messages were sent through bonfires, the gentile were lighting bonfires in order to confuse the Jews. Therefore they stopped using bonfires and started sending messengers.

💡 Sometimes, when important messages were sent, they used a code if a message was revealed to the enemy, he won't understand the context. The encryption methods are called cryptology.

💡 Nowadays because the use of the internet, the amount of letters are diminishing, but a huge number of a 150 billion letters each year.

Sweet Dreams

The book of Bereishit is full of dreams.

Let's take a look at Yosef's dreams at the beginning of Parashat Vayeshev.

Even though he was younger than most of his brothers, Yosef received special treatment from his father Yaakov. That was enough to make the brothers very jealous, but Yosef's dreams were the last straw. The brothers were furious when they heard them!

In the first dream, Yosef sees his brothers' sheaves of grain bowing down to his own sheaf. In the second dream he sees the sun, the moon and eleven stars bowing down to him. When Yosef tells his brothers about his dreams, the brothers realize what they mean. Yosef will eventually become their king and they will be his subjects! This makes them even angrier at Yosef than they were before. But why the brothers were so angry? Were the dreams Yosef's fault? Was there any way for him to stop them? Could he have controlled his dreams while he was asleep?

What is a dream?

In order to understand why the brothers were so angry, we have to understand what dreams actually are and why we dream at night.

The brain is one of the most important organs in our body. It is located in the head and controls everything that we do. Over the course of the day, the brain accumulates enormous amounts of information from the things that we learn, do, see and hear, like material that we learned at school, things that we saw on the way home, and stories that we heard from our friends. The brain has to organize all of this information in our memory so that we can remember it and use it later on. To get an idea of how this works, imagine that we have special "drawers" in our brain (just like the ones that you use to store your toys and clothes). Once the information is stored in the right drawers, we can use it later on. While we rest and sleep, the brain is busy arranging all of this information in the right drawers. While it organizes the information, it sees the events that happened during the day as if they were occurring right now. Even though we are asleep, we may feel like we are sitting in class or playing with our friends. These are our dreams.

When do we dream? All night long or only at certain times?

About 80 years ago, scientists discovered that sleep can be divided into stages. When we first fall asleep, we sleep lightly. Deeper sleep comes later. About two hours after we fall asleep we enter REM sleep, when most of our dreaming occurs. During this time, our eyes and eyelids move rapidly, and our brain locks down our muscles so that we don't physically respond to things that we see in our dreams. Once REM sleep ends, a new sleep cycle begins, starting with light sleep followed by deeper sleep and finally REM sleep. In total, we dream during about one-fifth of the time that we are asleep. If you get eight hours of sleep at night, for example, you will spend about an hour and a half in REM sleep, which is when people generally dream.

There are times when we remember every tiny detail of our dreams,. Other times we wake up and can't remember a thing.

What happens while we sleep? Why can't we always remember our dreams in the morning?

Scientists asked people to spend the night in a sleep lab so that they could study what happens while we sleep. The scientists wanted to study how the brain works while we sleep, so they connected these people to a special device that measures brain waves, and told them to go to sleep. They saw that the brain was very active during the first stage of sleep. They were surprised to discover that when they woke up the participants during REM sleep, they were able to recall their dreams in detail!

The scientists asked the participants to go back to sleep and then woke them up after REM sleep had ended. In this case, they couldn't remember their dreams. Scientists concluded that if we wake up during REM sleep, while we dream, we will remember our dream clearly. If we wake up at a different stage of sleep, chances are that we will not remember our dreams at all.

Sleeping laboratory

Scientists discovered that the brain has another job to do while we dream, other than organizing information. We all have different desires and aspirations. One person may want a certain game and another might want to go on a special trip. While we dream, the brain makes everything that we want, come true. We dream of getting that special game or going on the trip that we've been thinking so much about.

There is still a lot that we don't know about the brain. In fact, we know very little about how it works, including exactly what happens while we dream. But scientists are still trying to understand more about dreams and what they mean.

Let's get back to Yosef and his brothers. Remember the question that we asked earlier? Why did Yosef's dreams make his brothers so angry? Why did they blame Yosef?

The brothers apparently knew what scientists discovered thousands of years later. They understood that our dreams reflect the things that we do during the day, and express our inner hopes and desires. That is why they were so angry at Yosef. They felt that these were not just regular dreams. They meant that Yosef wanted to rule over them. Now it's easier to understand why they were so angry.

Sleep and dreaming are a very important part of our lives. While we sleep, our brain processes all of the information that we gathered during the day and makes room for the information that we will gather tomorrow. Our brain needs sleep, and the number of hours that we sleep has a direct effect on how well we do in school and with our friends. It is very important to get at least eight hours of sleep every night so that our body and our brain can get the rest that they need.

Interesting facts

💡 Many scientists think that we need dreams just as much as we need food and water. Just like people cannot survive for very long without food and water, they can't survive without dreams either.

💡 Many inventors got their best ideas while they were dreaming. A famous chemist named Kekulé was studying the structure of a certain material. Thanks to a clue that came to him in a dream, he managed to discover the structure that he was looking for.

💡 Our sages taught us that all dreams are our heart's reflections. If we think about good, happy things during the day, our dreams will be just as good!

How do We Preserve Food?

Yosef solves Pharaoh's dreams but does not stop there.

He adds to Pharaoh that he would take advantage of the years of famine, how? The solution is simple: In the seven years Pharaoh will keep eating in the camps, and in the years of famine Pharaoh and the Egyptians will be the only ones to have food. From all over the world they will come to Pharaoh. They will beg him to eat at any price he asks for. Thanks to Yosef's advice Pharaoh appoints him as his deputy and in charge of the whole food system in Egypt at the time of hunger. **There's a problem ahead of Yosef. We know that food that is left out of the refrigerator or freezer would spoil. How could Yosef preserve food more than seven years without spoiling?**

In order to understand. We need to know how the food doesn't spoil at all. This is how we would find out how to prevent the cracking and what method Yosef kept the food.

In ancient times most people cooked their own food, they harvest the wheat from the ground and prepare bread from them, and they slaughter the sheep and ate the meat and all other foods. The food had to be eaten immediately after its preparation since what was left was not edible after a few hours, the food was always fresh and delicious but it took a lot of work to prepare the food every day. If you want to bring home something that grew or was prepared at a distance it would be impossible to bring it home because it would spoil.

What is the cause of food getting spoiled to get quickly?

In the past there was a belief that there are small creatures who are created by themselves within the food and spoil it. Over the years they understood that since the creation of the world no creature has been created by itself, those who destroy the food, but rather are the bacteria and fungus that exist inside

the food and we do not see them. Small creatures and fungus love warm weather. It gets involved in the food and makes it to get spoiled. They multiply within it and lead to a spoiling or moldy taste. The insects and fungus love the warmth atmosphere and pleasant of the food. They are the cause that the food will get spoiled we understand that open air that are different type of insects.

Have you ever seen a fruit that after a while will work in the refrigerator seems to have shrunk or eaten? Did you see bread that was left out without covering for a long time until it seemed like something had been sprinkled on it with for a white vegetable color. What do we do in order to prevent that the food shouldn't be spoiled.

li addition, in the open air there are many insects and flying birds that can damage food, and sometimes wetness and dampness of the air also imprint the sacrifice of the food.

What do we do prevent the food from spoiling?

In order to prevent the freshness of the food. We found different ways to keep the food fresh, they found different ways to deal with decay and prevent it. Salt for example dries the food and also keeps it safe. Also sugar guards the freshness because keeps the food away. Also vinegar, oil and different materials. That way they were able to prepare in big quantities of food. To keep the food fresh they found different ways to deal with decay and prevent it.

More than that is ways to keep the food fresh to storage in dry places that air won't go through. The common method was to dig pits and inside to bury the food until it was used. Joseph the righteous man he was one of the first ones that was able to use this method and because he had a huge amount of grain, and the rot the whole pile of grain.

The righteous saint was probably one of the first to use the method because he had a small amount of grain and the grain will have not pile the whole amount of grain.

Commentators argued that Joseph also mixed some sand in the grain that helps to keep the grain fresh. Do you think that the idea will be successful? Everyone from all over the world came to Egypt to buy food, seven years after the food was collected.

What do you think? Saving food it is for our benefit.

It depends how you look at it. From one point. Nowadays there are many ways how to preserve food for a long period of time, fridge will conserve food for even longer. That way the insects won't damage the food.

Preservatives keeps the food to stay for a longer period of time. Also a different way that we preserve the food in plastic containers. In the other hand we get to eat food in a fresh manner that way losses its vitamin. Preservatives are not healthy.

How did Yosef know that in the past things people won't discover?
Yosef in Egypt didn't have a fridge also nobody knew about preservatives

He was smart and wise. He was able to discover different method how to conserve the food thinking method outside the box is to look how everybody is looking. Yosef understood that people in Egypt were starving and he needed to think how to preserve food for many years. He taught about many ideas that other people didn't think about. Yosef taught about saving the food in pits underneath the ground and adding different materials that will conserve the food.

According to his deeds Yosef was able to turned Egypt into a big Empire. We will learned from Yosef that sometimes we are stuck in different situations and we don't know how to solve them. To think about something very artistic outside the box in order to find and idea.

Interesting facts

💡 Different factories freeze the fruits after it was harvest and sold after few months. Even thought is not the season we will be able to find them in stores.

💡 On the time of Galut outside of Israel, wanted to eat during Tu Bishvat fruits from Israel. That were able to stay a long period of time. To dry them since then we have the custom to eat fruits on Tu bishvat.

💡 Not all the insects can damage the food. Some of them are in wine cheese yogurt.

I have a feeling that these are tears of sadness...

Ahhhhh!

Tears of Joy and Sadness

Yosef stays in Egypt for twenty two years, and he is the ruler.

Yosef's siblings don't recognize him, and they bring Binyamin the youngest of them all to Egypt at his request. When Yosef sees his little brother Binyamin, he can't keep back his secret anymore and reveals himself to his brothers and announces: "I am Yosef"! What an excitement, the missing brother is revealed in front of them! Yosef hugs his young brother Binyamin, and they both start to cry over each other's shoulders.

Why, in your opinion, did Yosef and Binyamin cry?

It is obvious to us how excited they were seeing each other, therefore they were crying out of excitement and joy. Chazal also explain that Yosef and Binyamin cried over the temples and the mishkan that would be established and destroyed in their property. If so, then Yosef and Binyamin also cried out of sadness and sorrow as well.

What do you think, can you tell why a person is crying, without asking them why? Have you ever been thinking why do we need tears? And where are the tears while we don't cry?

The human eye is just incredible.

It allows us to see from close and from distance a variety colors and shapes. In order to keep our eyes in place, G-d created several layers of protection: the first layer is the eye socket, a part of the skull that keeps the eye in place the eyeball inside (you can even touch above your eye and feel the bone – that's the eye socket). The second layer is the eyelids that closes every time there's a danger to the eyes. Whenever our brain senses a danger coming the eyelids shut immediately to protect it, even without paying attention. The third and the interesting layer is the tears.

In our eyes there are three types of tears.

The first type are tears that are meant to prevent a friction of our eyes and our eyelids. These type of tears are called basal tears and they are constantly on our eyes. These tears also assist the eyelids to shut easily and quickly when the eye senses a danger coming. The eye contains a gland that's called Lacrimal gland that constantly creates new tears; and the previous tears drain into a special tube below the eye straight into the Lacrimal sac, interesting to know that our eyes constantly shed tears without even noticing.

The second type, are tears that clean the eye and protects it from dirt and foreign bodies that get into the eye. Actually, the tears are a protection fluid against bacteria and also a cleaning fluid. Has a grain of sand ever get into your eye and you have instantly weep? It's an unpleasant feeling, right? Now we are sure that tears are a positive thing, because they basically clean the eye from dirt that gets into it.

The third type, are tears that drop in response to different types of moods, happiness, excitement, sadness or anger for example. These tears are called

Psychic tears. Have you ever wondered why do we cry when we are happy or sad?

In the past researchers thought that tears come out in order to cause other people to pay attention to us, if we were sad. As if the one who cries is saying: hey, look at me I am sad! Today, the researchers believe that the tears have another important role dealing with a bad mood or a bad feeling. While Psychic tears run down our eyes, they take out toxins and other chemicals, therefore the emotional mood is easier to deal with. Practically you can say that Psychic tears are a natural painkiller, just like a cure. Now we have seen that tears are very important for our body and our soul.

We learned that there are different types of tears. Tears that are formed constantly and moist our eye, Tears created when a foreign body or dirt enter the eye, and tears that are the result of an emotional state.

Tear researchers conducted an interesting experiment.

They ask a few people to cry, each one for a different reason. The tears were brought to a laboratory. In the laboratory the test revealed something special: Each sort of tears, which were composed from different causes of crying, was composed from different components.

In an additional experiment, they took pictures of the tears from all the sorts and they saw in the tiny structure of the tears witch you can see only through a microscope that increases the image a lot. What the researchers revealed was unusual: not only that each and every sort of tears has its own components, but they also look different. The particles of tears from different sorts have different shapes. For example the tears of joy have a cheerful jumpy structure, and tears of anger and sadness have a straight and fixed structure. Amazing, right?

If we could examine the tears of Yosef and Binyamin we would surely had found tears of different kind: Tears of joy and excitement about the happy encounter, and also tears of sorrow for the future of the Jewish people. A future that will perceive difficulties and destruction.

We have asked at the beginning: Could we find out the reason of crying without asking him? The answer is of course! Different type of tears have different type of structure.

The human body is the most interesting machine in the world that works constantly while we're awake and asleep, without even noticing.

G-d created us mechanisms that will protect our body parts, like the tears that protect our eyes. Furthermore, we have in our body different types of pain killer materials that cure us from different types of illnesses, even when we don't feel them. When we are happy or sad and the tears fall by itself, it testifies that our body works properly, the body supplies our eyes protection, and also helps itself going through the special state it's in.

Interesting facts

💡 Why do our eyes tear when we cut an onion? When cutting it, the onion releases a specific substance witch the eyes identifies as a dangerous factor that wants to harm it. In order to wash down the substance, the body releases tears.

💡 The Canadian astronaut Chris Hadfield filmed a video in space and shows how tears are like in space. Turns out they just stay around the eyes and do not leak down the cheeks.

💡 If we gather our tears throughout a full year we could be able to fill big bottles, that's about 120 litters a year.

Row Row Row Your Boat

> **Zevulun shall dwell by seashores. He shall be at the ships harbor, and his end is at Sidon.**

n Yaakov's blessings to his sons, he allots to Zevulun the trade of seamanship/sailing. Indeed, once the Jews enter the land of Israel, Zevulun receives plots of land near the Mediterranean and along the shores of the Galilee. In addition, Yisasschar and Zevulun form a partnership: The tribe of Yisasschar will learn Torah for the tribe of Zevulun, while the tribe of Zevulun financially provides for the tribe of Yisasschar in return.

Why does the tribe of Zevulun require a special blessing for its trade [for the trade of seamanship]? How come this special partnership is specifically with the tribe of Yisasschar and not with any other tribe?

Today, as well as In earlier days, the ocean has a significant role in transferring goods from one place to another. Usually sea goers were employed by merchant fleets which are similar to the moving companies we have today[we have nowadays?]. Merchant fleets transferred goods that came from far away lands, from one place to another, and sold them. The transferring of goods from one place to another usually is beneficial. Items commonly found in Israel, take dates for example, will most likely be sold in Israel at a low cost. However in far away lands, where dates dont grow, goods can be sold for a higher price. Furthermore, lots of things are easier to transfer by sea as opposed to by land.

Do you have an idea what may be easier to be transferred by sea?

Large Cedar trees were used in the construction of The Temple. These trees dont grow in Israel but rather in Lebenon, which lies north of Israel. Hiram the King of Tyre sold these trees, needed for the construction of The Temple, to King Solomon. However, how were they transferred to Jerusalem?

Being that trees can float, The King of Tyres slaves placed them in the ocean and a ship carried them to the shores of Israel. From there, the journey to Jerusalem is short.

Apart from transferring goods, the voyages were used to transfer knowledge [information] between people and countries. When seagoers would reach new places they would take back with them new inventions or qualified people who knew how to do special[significant\certain?] things. With the conclusion of a journey they would enrich their land with science and knowledge. Thus[As a result\because of this?] King Solomon and many other kings invested a lot of money in building ships and qualifying men to sail in order to bring back goods and knowledge from faraway places.

If the idea is so simple, Why arent ships constantly sailing from country to country?

With every opportunity there are risks. In the past sailing the seas was very dangerous. Most ships were made from wood and would navigate with the help of wind. As a result, journeys by sea would last months with rocking, strong storms, waves that were twenty meters high, pirates that sought out ships to steal their cargo and constant battle against the mighty seas.

Without a doubt seagoers, especially The Zevelun tribe, were in need of a special blessing in order to complete the long [and tedious] journey successfully. Today, as well as in the past, one who returns from a long journey at sea recites Bircat Hagomel.

At the end of a journey at sea, if the ship survived its obstacles and reached its destination, Its merchants could sell their goods at a high price and make a lot of money. Likewise, they were able to buy special items unattainable in Israel, like certain spices or expensive textiles, and sell them for a lot of money upon their return.

Nowadays, most of the worlds trade passes through sea despite there being more than enough planes and trucks. Although the journey is long and ships are slow, it is the cheapest and most efficient way to transfer goods. Transferring things by plane, especially heavy goods, is more costly. Transferring goods, such as the likes of cars from Japan, oil from China, furniture from Italy and wheat from America; will most likely be done by sea. Carrier ships today are enormous and are able to hold heavy cargo, even up to 250,000 tons! A weight that is equal to that of half the human population.

Today, trade by sea is very import to Israel as it is unable to transfer cargo by land or sky to Europe or Asia through Arab countries.

Today, as in the past, sea goers discover new places and make an honorable profit from trade. However, they leave their homes for long periods of time and their work is difficult and dangerous. Even with newer ships sailing the world can take weeks, even months. As a result sea goers don't always have the ability to invest time into their children's studies and education.

Worlds largest carrier ship. Photo by: Maersk Line

Now the partnership between the tribes of Yisasschar and Zevulun is understood. The Yisasschar tribe will be responsible for The Zevulun Tribes children's education whilst they are at sea; In return, the Zevulun Tribe will return plentiful from their trips and will be able to provide for and fill the needs of The Yisasschar tribe.

Partnership / Cooperation:
There are times when we have many things to do and aren't always able to do them on our own. It is important we know how to ask for help from friends or family as well as knowing when to offer it to those in need. For instance, if our parents are busy in the kitchen, we can offer help tidying up the house. If the housework is plentiful we can get family members to work together and help out, just like Yisasschar and Zevulun helped each other. When we work together, the workload will be easier and more pleasant.

Interesting facts

💡 In order for a ship to dock at a harbor the depth of the water must be at least twelve meters. Ships that are full of cargo are heavy and sink in water, so at times they dock at sea and small boats bring the cargo to shore.

💡 One of the most famous ships is the Titanic, which was built in England in 1912 and was considered unsinkable. On its first voyage to America it hit an iceberg and sunk. About 1,500 passengers died in the accident.

💡 More than ninety percent of worldwide trade is done with assistance of ships.

About the authors:

Nati Ben David: A teacher and educator, writes and edits educational content.

Avraham Nativ: An electronics engineer. Received a physics degree.

Levi Tsehmeister: Industrial and management engineer.

Contact the authors:

maasebereshitbook@gmail.com